P9-AFD-800

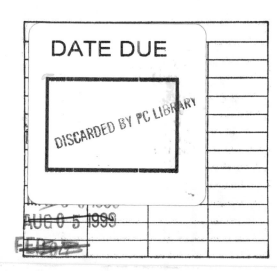

SHAKESPEARE ALLUSIONS
AND PARALLELS

BY

A. BRUCE BLACK

and

ROBERT METCALF SMITH, Ph.D.

Professor of English
Lehigh University

AMS PRESS
NEW YORK

Reprinted from the edition of 1931, Bethlehem

First AMS EDITION published 1971

Manufactured in the United States of America

International Standard Book Number: 0-404-00893-3

Library of Congress Catalog Number: 78-113559

AMS PRESS INC.
NEW YORK, N.Y. 10003

FOREWORD BY THE EDITOR

The allusions and parallels printed in this pamphlet have been selected by the editor from more than five hundred passages submitted to him by Mr. A. Bruce Black of Bloomsburg, Pennsylvania. They are, with a few exceptions, not the editor's, but Mr. Black's discoveries, the fruit of many years of intensive reading in his valuable library of Shakespeare allusion books. Mr. Black's remarkable associative memory enables him not only to discover like expressions and ideas throughout English poetry, but to locate them readily in the works, particularly of Shakespeare and his successors. The 566 passages from which these have been selected comprise all shades and degrees of likeness whether of thought or expression; they range all the way from maxims and phraseology that were current coin in the seventeenth century, slight verbal similarities, coincidences or faint echoes of Shakespearean thought or style, from doubtful, possible, probable, or unconscious borrowings, to obvious parallels and outright references not only to Shakespeare's characters and plays, but to Shakespeare himself.

The first task of the editor was to decide what should be included and what rejected. For this purpose he accepted the standard set by John Munro and his predecessors and successors.

As in Munro's volumes or in those collections made by his predecessors, for example, *The Centurie of Prayse,* by Clement Ingleby, and additions by Furnivall, L. Toulmin Smith, and other members of the

iii

New Shakespeare Society, certain border line cases are inevitably open to differences of opinion. Perhaps another editor would have selected from the 566 passages some that I have discarded, and would have rejected others that I have included.

After the editor had reduced the number of probable and actual allusions and parallels to seventy-eight, he submitted them for judgment to Dr. Samuel A. Tannenbaum and to Dr. Henry W. Wells of Columbia University. Out of seventy-eight, these scholars accepted forty-one, discarded fifteen, and disagreed upon twenty-two — five of which Dr. Tannenbaum allowed, as against Dr. Wells' seventeen. Confronted with these marked differences of opinion, the editor has assumed responsibility for all final decisions; and the reader interested in Shakespeare allusions and parallels is privileged to enjoy the pleasures of both dissent and agreement. My own contributions to these allusions are several references to Shakespeare and his plays that appeared in *The Athenian Mercury* (March 17, 1691—June 14, 1697) and were reprinted in *The Athenian Oracle* during the early years of the eighteenth century.

The second task of the editor has been to ascertain whether these passages had been noted before. So far as he has been able to discover they have not been published. Munro's *Shakespeare Allusion Book,* 1909 and his Supplement of 1916 (*Modern Philology* xiii p. 129ff.) have been supplemented recently by G. Thorn-Drury's two valuable pamphlets of *Seventeenth Century Allusions,* issued in 1921 and 1924 by Dobell. From time to time other allusions have appeared in such learned periodicals as the *Shakespeare*

Jahrbuch, Modern Language Notes, Notes and Queries, and the *Literary Supplement* of the *London Times.* Eventually, as Mr. Black suggests in his preface, another gathering to date, like that of Munro's may be necessary.

Longer and more minute analyses to substantiate the assimilation of Shakespeare's thought and style by his successors have appeared in such studies as Professor Alwin Thaler's "Shakespeare and Sir Thomas Browne" and "The Shakespearian Element in Milton" in *Shakespeare's Silences* (Harvard University Press, 1929) and in Professor George Coffin Taylor's "Shakespeare and Milton Again" (*Studies in Philology* xxiii, 1926, 189-199). As Professor Thaler wisely suggests, the allusion hunter must constantly remember Sir Thomas Browne's warning that the likeness between almost any two authors may be merely the product of "conceits and expressions common unto them with others, and that not by *imitation* but *coincidence and concurrence* of imagination upon harmony of production." On the other hand, I think Professor Thaler is equally justified in his belief that "the skeptics who would laugh out of court anything and everything that they can manage to label parallel-chasing need to be reminded that all loose generalizations are false, including theirs, and that in the study of imaginative literature anyone whose eyes and ears are open constantly meets with analogies, parallelisms, echoes of thought or language, which sometimes, if in a given instance one unwarily pauses to look or listen more closely, become not the pursued but the pursuers." (Op. cit. p. 114-115.)

Mr. Black and I herewith acknowledge our indebtedness to the kindness, patience, and judgment of Dr. Tannenbaum and Dr. Wells; and also to the labors of my student assistant, Mr. Kenneth K. Kost, who has prepared the index and ably performed much of the detail work.

ROBERT METCALF SMITH,
Bethlehem, Pennsylvania.

PREFATORY NOTE

The allusions and parallels to Shakespeare and his works in this monograph are neither in the publications of Munro nor in subsequent collections published by Dobell of London; and so far as I know none of them (with the exception of one that I discovered in 1927 and sent to several newspapers and magazines in both America and Europe) has ever been noted. I realize, however, that many learned periodicals in Europe, particularly in England and Germany, are frequently printing hitherto unnoticed Shakespeare allusions, and that it is quite possible to duplicate unwittingly what some one else has discovered. To guard against such errors I have availed myself of the scholar's apparatus at the command of Professor Smith, for in his search he tells me he has come upon instances of allusions repeatedly printed as independent discoveries.

Hitherto unnoticed Shakespeare allusions should be sent at once to the leading papers and periodicals, for these "little grains of scholarship," as they have appropriately been called, are sometimes of great value not only to scholars, but also to collectors of Shakespeareana. As an illustration — a short time after a New York paper published one of my allusions, the late Mr. Henry Clay Folger wrote to me that he had advertised in London for a copy of the book containing it, and thanked me for the dissemination of the information. Mr. A. W. Pollard of the British Museum, after reading the allusion in one of the London papers, wrote to me that he had never seen it before; and I also received a letter of thanks from Oxford University. In April, 1930, I received a letter of thanks from the Library of Congress for calling attention to a Shakespeare allusion in Philipott's *Villare Cantianum,* 1659, offered in a recent English catalogue for only ten shillings; and when I notified another English book dealer who was listing another copy at twelve shillings six pence, he raised his price three months later to five pounds five shillings and reprinted in his catalogue the allusion to Prince Hal and Falstaff.

A new Shakespeare Allusion Book, containing all allusions to date, should be published. Such a work, on account of the many new allusions discovered since the last contributions of Munro and G. Thorn-Drury, would add to the already incontrovertible proof that Shakespeare received more reference and more praise from contemporary writers than any other dramatist, and that throughout the seventeenth century he was recognized, as he has been ever since, as the master spirit of mankind. Moreover, these passages, and in my opinion a great many that Professor Smith has not included, are additional testimony to the way Shakespeare permeated in thought and language the literature of the seventeenth century.

Almost all of my reading in the literature of the period has been from the first or early editions of Shakespeare allusion books and other volumes that I have collected and read for over thirty-five years.

A. BRUCE BLACK,
Bloomsburg, Pennsylvania.

September, 1929.

[Shakespeare references in this study are based upon the Globe text; those to Beaumont and Fletcher, upon the Darley edition of 1839; those to other Jacobean dramatists, upon *The Mermaid Series;* and those to other authors, from original or early editions as specified.]

THOMAS DEKKER (1599)

I'll Be A Park

HAM. A deer more dear is found within this place.
ROSE. But not the deer, sir, which you had in chase.
HAM. I chased the deer, but this dear chaseth me.
ROSE. The strangest hunting that ever I see. But
where's your park?
HAM. 'Tis here: O stay!
ROSE. Impale me, and then I will not stray.

The Shoemaker's Holiday (II, 5, 40-47)

Fondling, she saith, since I have hemm'd thee here
Within the circuit of this ivory pale,
I'll be a park, and thou shalt be my deer.

Venus and Adonis (lines 229-231)

[Thomas Heywood in *The Fayre Maid of the Exchange*, 1607,
also quotes this passage from *Venus and Adonis*, as does Thomas
Durfey in *The Virtuous Wife*, 1680. Munro I, 177, II, 256. For
another Shakespeare allusion in Dekker's play, see Munro I, 64.]

JOHN MARSTON (1602)

The Wolf Behowls The Moon

Now barks the wolf against the full-cheek'd moon;
Now lions half-clam'd entrails roar for food;
Now croaks the toad, and night-crows screech aloud,
Fluttering 'bout casements of departed souls;
Now gapes the graves and through their yawns let
    loose
Imprison'd spirits to revisit earth.

*II Antonio and Mellida, Antonio's
Revenge* (III, 2, 184-189)

Now the hungry lion roars,
And the wolf behowls the moon;
Whilst the heavy plowman snores,
    All with weary task fordone.
Now the wasted brands do glow,
    Whilst the screech-owl, screeching loud,
Puts the wretch that lies in woe
    In remembrance of a shroud.
Now it is the time of night
    That the graves all gaping wide,
Every one lets forth his sprite,
    In the church-way paths to glide.

Midsummer Night's Dream (V, 1, 378-389)

[Another allusion in *Antonio and Mellida*, Munro I, 108.]

2

HUGH HOLLAND (1603)

Black Men Seem Pearls

Is it because that in faire women's eyes
Black men seeme pearles?

Pancharis, Book 1

Black men are pearls in beauteous ladies' eyes.

Two Gentlemen of Verona (V, 2, 12)

[See J. P. Collier's *Biographical Account of Early English Literature,* II, 445.]

THOMAS DEKKER AND THOMAS MIDDLETON (1604)

His Vocation

If it be my vocation to swear, every man in his vocation:
I hope my betters swear and damn themselves, and why should
Not I?

I The Honest Whore (III, 2, 61-62)

Why, Hal, 'tis my vocation, Hal; 'tis no sin for a man to labour in his vocation.

I Henry IV (I, 2, 116-117)

[For many other allusions in this play, see Munro I, 65-6.]

THOMAS DEKKER (1608)

Poor Tom Is A Cold

Onely to make you beleeve he is out of his wits: he calls himselfe by the name of Poore Tom, and comming neere any body, cryes out, Poore Tom is a cold.

The Bel-Man of London,—

An Abraham-man (lines 13-17)

Bless thy five wits! Tom's a-cold—O, do de, do de, do de. Bless thee from whirlwinds, star-blasting, and taking! Do Poor Tom some charity, whom the foul fiend vexes.

King Lear (III, 4, 59-62)

THOMAS HEYWOOD (1608)

Love Will Creep

Now what is love I will you show:
A thing that creeps and cannot go,

The Rape of Lucrece (II, 1, 115-116)

Ay, gentle Thurio: for you know that love
Will creep in service where it cannot go.

Two Gentlemen of Verona (IV, 2, 19-20)

[Prof. G. C. Moore Smith (*Notes and Queries,* Eleventh
Series, VIII, p. 155) believes the phrase a proverb, as it occurs
in *Wily Beguiled,* and in a marginal note of Gabriel Harvey's
in a book of his now in the Saffron Walden Museum. G. Thorn-
Drury finds it also in *The Drunkard's Character, N. & Q.,* op. cit.
p. 86.]

FRANCIS BEAUMONT AND JOHN FLETCHER (c. 1609)

Discourse and Reason

Why should a man, that has discourse and reason,
And knows how near he loses all in these things,
Covet to have his wishes satisfied?

The Coxcomb (IV, 8, 7-9)

O God! a beast, that wants discourse of reason,
Would have mourned longer.

Hamlet (I, 2, 150-151)

JOHN FLETCHER (c. 1609)

I Am Mortal

Is there in me, to draw submission
From this rude man and beast? Sure I am mortal:
The daughter of a shepherd; he was mortal,
And she that bore me mortal: prick my hand
And it will bleed; A fever shakes me, and
The self-same wind that makes the young lambs
    shrink,
Makes me a-cold: My fear says I am mortal.

The Faithful Shepherdess (I, 1, 104-109)

I am a Jew. Hath not a Jew eyes? hath not a
Jew hands, organs, dimensions, senses, affections,
passions? fed with the same food, hurt with the same
weapons, subject to the same diseases, healed by the
same means, warmed and cooled by the same winter
and summer, as a Christian is? If you prick us, do
we not bleed? if you tickle us, do we not laugh? if
you poison us, do we not die? and if you wrong us,
shall we not revenge?

Merchant of Venice (III, 1, 64-73)

CHRISTOPHER BROOKE (1614)

Stern Alarums

Yet now (secure) Edward enjoy'd the crowne.
Warre's stern alarums heere began to cease;
Bankes turned to pillows, fields to beds of downe,
And boysterous armes to silken robes of peace.

The Ghost of Richard the Third (Part II, 81-84)

Our stern alarums changed to merry meetings,
Our dreadful marches to delightful measures.

Richard III (1, 1, 7-8)

[For other allusions to *Richard III* from this work, see Munro
I, 249-250.]

RICHARD BRAITHWAITE (1615)

Not Made To Court A Looking Glass

I that neuer loued was,
Nor could court a looking-glasse.

A Strappado for the Diuell.
Frankie's Anatomie 1615, page 79.

But I, that am not shaped for sportive tricks,
Nor made to court an amorous looking-glass.

Richard III (I, 1, 14-15)

[For other allusions in *A Strappado for the Diuell*, see Munro I, 256-257.]

BEAUMONT AND FLETCHER AND OTHERS (1615)

A Long Farewell

Farewell!
To all our happiness, a long farewell!

Cupid's Revenge (IV, 4, 26-27)

So farewell to the little good you bear me.
Farewell! a long farewell, to all my greatness!

Henry VIII (III, 2, 350-351)

BEAUMONT AND FLETCHER AND OTHERS (before 1616?)

A Little Pin

May superstition choak them! What's this toy,
Or idol they so reverence, but a spunge
Fill'd with the king's waste moisture, or a bag
Blown with the breath of greatness? When the hand
Of wrath shall squeeze it, or a little pin
Prick but the windy outside, down falls all
And leaves him nought but despised emptiness.

The Faithful Friends (IV, 3, 53-58)

Comes at the last and with a little pin
Bores through his castle wall, and—farewell king!

Richard II (III, 2, 169-170)

12

BEAUMONT AND FLETCHER AND OTHERS (before 1616?)

For Soft Delights

Had you viewed him
As he went drooping through the city-gates,
You might have seen his heart there charactered;
He looked as if with joy he could have changed
His march for a soft measure, his loud drum
For a still quavering lute,
His waving colours for a lady's scarf,
And his stiff armour for a masquing suit.

The Faithful Friends (II, 1, 75-82)

Now are our brows bound with victorious wreaths;
Our bruised arms hung up for monuments;
Our stern alarums changed to merry meetings,
Our dreadful marches to delightful measures.
Grim-visaged war hath smooth'd his wrinkled front;
And now,—instead of mounting barbed steeds
To fright the souls of fearful adversaries,
He capers nimbly in a lady's chamber
To the lascivious pleasing of a lute.

Richard III (I, 1, 5-13)

NATHANIEL FIELD (1618)

Drowned in Wine

TEARCHAPS. We'll down into the cellar, and drown thee in a butt of Malmsey, and hew all the hogsheads in pieces.

WHOREBANG. Hang him rogue, shall he die as honourable as the Duke of Clarence?

Amends For Ladies, 1618 (III, 4, 2-6)

FIRST MURDERER. Take that, and that: if all this will not do, (*Stabs him.*)
I'll drown you in the malmsey-butt within.

Richard III, (I, 4, 276-277)

[See also Munro I, 270.]

14

FRANCIS BEAUMONT AND JOHN FLETCHER (1619)

False As Hell

GOBRIAS. Sir, it is she.
ARBACES. 'Tis false.
GOBRIAS. Is it?
ARBACES. As hell! By heaven, as false as hell!

A King and No King (III, 1, 144-147)

OTHELLO. Swear thou art honest.
DESDEMONA. Heaven doth truly know it.
OTHELLO. Heaven truly knows that thou art false as
hell.

Othello (IV, 2, 37-39)

[See also Munro I, 197.]

15

JOHN FLETCHER AND PHILIP MASSINGER (c. 1620, Folio 1647)

All the Perfumes in Arabia

I'll tell thee all the gums in sweet Arabia
Are not sufficient, were they burnt about thee,
To purge the scent of a rank rascal from thee.

The False One (III, 2, 87-89)

Here's the smell of the blood still: all the perfumes
of Arabia will not sweeten this little hand.

Macbeth (V, 1, 56-58)

THOMAS DEKKER AND OTHERS
(1621, published 1658)

Get you to your nunnery;

The Witch of Edmonton (I, 1, 262)

Get thee to a nunnery!

Hamlet (III, 1, 122)

[See also Munro, *Mod. Phil.* XIII, p. 141.]

THOMAS DEKKER AND OTHERS
(1621, published 1658)

I Did Not Think To Shed A Tear

Go thy ways; I did not think to have shed one tear for thee, but thou hast made me water my plants spite of my heart.

The Witch of Edmonton (V, 2, 176-178)

Cromwell, I did not think to shed a tear
In all my miseries; but thou hast forced me,
Out of thy honest truth, to play the woman.

Henry VIII (III, 2, 429-431)

THOMAS DEKKER AND OTHERS
(1621, published 1658)

What Charms

Strike, do!—and withered may that hand and arm
Whose blows have lamed me drop from the rotten
    trunk.
Abuse me! beat me! call me hag and witch!
What is the name, where and by what art learned,
What spells, what charms, or invocations,
May the thing called Familiar be purchased?

The Witch of Edmonton (II, 1, 31-36)

I will a round unvarnish'd tale deliver
Of my whole course of love; what drugs, what charms,
What conjuration and what mighty magic,
For such proceeding I am charged withal,
I won his daughter.

Othello (I, 3, 90-94)

JOHN FLETCHER (1621, Folio 1647)

Mad Men In England

ALPHONSO. How comes this English madman here?
MASTER. Alas, that is no question; they are mad every-
    where, sir.

The Pilgrim (IV, 3, 58-59)

I. CLOWN. It was the very day that young Hamlet was
    born, he that is mad, and sent into England.
HAMLET. Ay, marry, why was he sent into England?
I. CLOWN. Why, because he was mad; he shall recover
    his wits there; or, if he do not, it's no great matter
    there.
HAMLET. Why?
I. CLOWN. 'Twill not be seen in him there; there the
    men are as mad as he.

Hamlet (V, 1, 162-170)

JOHN WEBSTER (1623)

Two Towels

For two yeares together, I wore two Towells in
stead of a shirt, with a knot on the shoulder, after the
fashion of a Romaine Mantle:

The Duchess of Malfi (I, 1, 36-38)

There's but a shirt and a half in all my company;
and the half shirt is two napkins tacked together and
thrown over the shoulders like an herald's coat without sleeves;

I Henry IV (IV, 2, 48-52)

[See also Munro I, 117 ff.]

JOHN WEBSTER (1623)

The Means Whereby I Live

I cannot thinke, they meane well to your life,
That doe deprive you of your meanes of life,
Your living.

The Duchess of Malfi (V, 1, 11-13)

You take my house when you do take the prop
That doth sustain my house; You take my life
When you do take the means whereby I live.

Merchant of Venice (IV, 1, 375-378)

GEORGE WITHERS (1628)

Against A Sea of Troubles

Befool'd my wisdome; of much joy bereft me;
Within the *Sea* of troubles left me.

Brittain's Remembrancer, Canto V, p.159

Or to take arms against a sea of troubles,

Hamlet (III, 1, 59)

GEORGE WITHERS (1628)

A Rank Weed

For, when a noysome weed is seene to sprout,
She shall, at thy appointment, weed him out.

> *Brittain's Remembrancer,* 1628, Canto 1, p. 38

He's a rank weed, Sir Thomas, and we must root him
out.

> *Henry VIII* (V, 1, 52-53)

WILLIAM STRODE (1602-1645)

Look How The Morn

Looke how the russet morne exceeds the night.

> *On Gray Eyes,* Dobell's Edition
> of Strode, 1908, p. 35, l. 1.

But, look, the morn, in russet mantle clad,
Walks o'er the dew of yon high eastward hill.

> *Hamlet* (I, 1, 166-167)

JOHN FLETCHER AND JAMES SHIRLEY.
(c. 1633, published 1640)

Married to Her Grave

You had better marry her to her grave a great deal.

The Night-Walker (I, 3, 46)

I would the fool were married to her grave!

Romeo and Juliet (III, 5, 141)

JOHN FORD (1633)

When The Wind Blows Southerly

GRAUSIS. I am thick of hearing,
   Still, when the wind blows southerly.

*   *   *   *   *   *   *   *

Pray. speak louder. Sure, sure the wind blows
   south still.
PENTHEA. Thou prat'st madly.

The Broken Heart (II, 1, 137-138 and 144-145)

I am but mad north-north-west: when the wind is
southerly I know a hawk from a handsaw.

Hamlet (II, 2, 394-395)

27

JOHN FORD (1633)

Dying A Good Old Man

You may live well, and die a good old man.

The Broken Heart (IV, 2, 164)

[*aside*] Amen; and make me die a good old man!
That is the butt-end of a mother's blessing:
I marvel why her grace did leave it out.

Richard III (II, 2, 109-111)

SIR FRANCIS KYNASTON (1635)

Ways Be Foul

Nor is cold Winter yet at all
Less frolicke, then the wanton Spring:
The Robin red Brests in the Hall
Picking up crummes at Christmas sing
When winds blow cold, the wayes be fowle
In Barnes and sheepe coates sits the Owle,
Whose note the husbandman delights
When as shee hoots in frosty nights.

Corona Minervae, or a Masque Presented before Prince Charles,
His Highness the Duke of Yorke his brother, and the Lady Mary
his Sister, the 27th of February, at the Colledge of the Museum
Minervae. London, Printed for William Sharres, 1635. (I, 1, 10-
18.)

When icicles hang by the wall
And Dick the shepherd blows his nail
And Tom bears logs into the hall
And milk comes frozen home in pail,
When blood is nipp'd and ways be foul,
Then nightly sings the staring owl, Tu-whit;
Tu who, a merry note,
While greasy Joan doth keel the pot.

Love's Labour's Lost (V, 2, 922-930)

[See Winstanley's version in *Poor Robin,* 1670; G. Thorn-
Drury, *More Seventeenth Century Allusions,* 1924, p. 8.]

THOMAS RANDOLPH (1638)

ORGILUS. Dags and Pistolls!
    To bite his thumb at me!
AORGUS. Why should not any man
    Bite his own thumb?
ORGILUS. At me? were I a sword
    To see men bite their thumbs — Rapiers and
    Daggers!

The Muses Looking Glass (III, 5, 2-7)

SAMPSON. I will bite my thumb at them; which is a
    disgrace to them, if they bear it.
ABRAM. Do you bite your thumb at us, sir?
SAMPSON. I do bite my thumb, sir.
ABRAM. Do you bite your thumb at us, sir?

*   *   *   *   *   *   *   *

SAMPSON. No, sir, I do not bite my thumb at you, sir,
    but I bite my thumb, sir.

Romeo and Juliet (I, 1, 48-58)

ABRAHAM COWLEY (1646)

I Will See Thee At Philippi

Ill fate assum'd a body thee t' affright,
And wrapped itself i' the terrors of the night:
"I'll meet thee at Philippi," said the sprite.

Brutus, An Ode (lines 48-50)

BRUTUS. Why comest thou?
GHOST. To tell thee thou shalt see me at Philippi.

Julius Caesar (IV, 3, 283-284)

[See also Munro, *Mod. Phil.* XIII, p. 153.]

31

RICHARD FANSHAWE (1647)

(Poor Soul) Concealment like a worm i' th' bud,
Lies in her Damask cheek sucking the bloud.

Translation of Guarini's Pastor Fido, 1647, p. 36

A blank, my lord. She never told her love,
But let concealment, like a worm i' the bud,
Feed on her damask cheek:

Twelfth Night (II, 4, 114-116)

JOHN FLETCHER AND PHILIP MASSINGER (Folio 1647)

Discourse and Reason

Shall I then, that have reason and discourse,
That tell me all I can do is too little,
Be more unnatural than a silly bird?

The Spanish Curate (I, 2, 83-85)

O God! a beast, that wants discourse of reason,
Would have mourn'd longer.

Hamlet (I, 2, 150-151)

JOHN FLETCHER AND PHILIP MASSINGER (1647)

Bitter Bread of Banishment

Does she suffer so much for me,
For me unworthy, and shall I decline
Eating the bitter bread of banishment,
The course of justice, to draw out a life?

The Lover's Progress (V, 1, 95-98)

And sigh'd my English breath in foreign clouds,
Eating the bitter bread of banishment;
Whilst you have fed upon my signories.

Richard II (III, 1, 19-22)

ABRAHAM COWLEY (1650)

To Be Or Not To Be

What's somebody, or nobody?
In all the cobwebs of the schoolmen's trade,
We no such nice distinction woven see,
As 'tis "to be," or "not to be."

Life and Fame (lines 3-6)

To be, or not to be:

Hamlet (III, 1, 56)

ARTHUR WILSON (1653)

An. Reg. 4. An. Christi 1606

In *July* this year the King of *Danemark* (brother to the *Queen*) came in person as a *visitor,* where he found their shakings somewhat setled, their Terrors abated, and met with not onely all those varieties that Riches, Power, and Plenty are capable to produce for *satisfaction,* where *will* and *affection* are the *dispensers,* but he beheld with admiration the *stately Theatre,* whereon the *Danes* for many hundred of yeares had acted their bloody parts: But how he resented their *Exit,* or the last *Act* of that black *Tragedy,* wherein his Country lost her interest,[1] some *Divine Power,* that searches the capacious hearts of *Princes* can onely discover. This *short Moneth* of his stay carryed with it as pleasing a countenance on every side, and their *Recreations* and *Pastimes,* flew as high a flight, as *Love* mounted upon the wings of *art* and *fancie,* the sutable *nature* of the *soason,* or Times swift foot could possibly arrive at. The Court, City, and some parts of the Country, with Banquettings, Masks, Dancings, Tiltings, Barriers, and other Gallantry (besides the manly Sports of Wreastling, and the brutish Sports of baything Wild-beasts) swelled to such a greatness, as if there were an intention in every particular man, this way to have blown up himself.

> *THE HISTORY OF GREAT BRITAIN,* Being The Life and Reign of KING JAMES THE FIRST, Relating To what passed from his first Accesse to the Crown, till his Death. By ARTHUR WILSON, Esq., LONDON, Printed for *Richard Lownds,* and are to be sold at the Sign of the *White Lion* near Saint *Paul's* little North dore. 1653, page 33.

[1A possible reference to *Hamlet* as one of the two plays given by the King's Men at Greenwich before King James and the King of Denmark, July 18-24, 1606. For three plays, July-August 1606, "John Heminges one of his Mates Players" received £30 by warrant drawn Oct. 18. See E. K. Chambers, *Elizabethan Stage,* IV, 121, 173; *William Shakespeare,* II, 333. For this allusion we are indebted to David A. Randall of The Brickrow Bookshop, New York City.]

EDMUND GAYTON (1654)

Cain's Jaw-Bone

If you came fortified with Cain's jawbone, and will maintaine a challenge good against your own brother, not of the sword only, but nature, then you are of the right flame, a brother of the jaw-bone.

Notes Upon Don Quixote,
London, 1654, Book IV, p. 177

That skull had a tongue in it, and could sing once: how the knave jowls it to the ground, as if it were Cain's jaw-bone, that did the first murder!

Hamlet (V, 1, 83-86)

[For other allusions in this work, see Munro II, 32, 36, 37; also the article by J. K. Bonnell on *Cain's Jaw Bone, P. M. L. A.* XXXIX, 1924.]

JASPER MAYNE (1659)

I've the strangest company of Voluntaries;
All Gentlemen of the Hedges, and Highwaies.
I doe command an Hospital. Of fifty
But two have Shirts among 'em.

The Amorous Warre, 1659, p. 27 (II, 6, 8-11)

There's but a shirt and a half in all my company;
and the half-shirt is two napkins tacked together and
thrown over the shoulders like an herald's coat without sleeves; and the shirt, to say the truth, stolen from
my host at Saint Alban's, or the red-nose innkeeper
of Daventry. But that's all one; they'll find linen
enough on every hedge.

I Henry IV (IV, 2, 47-53)

WILLIAM WYCHERLEY (1661-2)

Crabbed Age And Youth

MRS. CAUTION. I wish the French levity of this young man may agree with your father's Spanish gravity. HIPPOLITA. Just as your crabbed old age and my youth agree.

The Gentleman Dancing Master (I, 1, 258-261)

Crabbed age and youth cannot live together.

Passionate Pilgrim (Stanza XII, 157)

SIR WILLIAM DUGDALE (1664)

"These following verses were made by William Shakespeare, the late famous tragedian." These verses according to Dugdale are on the east and the west ends of the tomb of Thomas Stanley, Knight.

'Aske who lyes here, but do not weepe;
He is not dead, he doth but sleepe.
This stony register is for his bones,
His fame is more perpetual than these stones:
And his own goodness, with himself being gone,
Shall live, when earthly monument is none.'

———

'Not monumental stone preserves our fame,
Nor skye-aspiring pyramids our name.
The memory of him for whom this stands,
Shall out-live marble, and defacer's hands.
When all to time's consumption shall be given,
Stanley, for whom this stands, shall stand in heaven.'

[Quoted from Malone who refers to Dugdale's collection of Epitaphs, 1664, now remaining in the College of Arms, Chap. XXXV, fol. 20. (Drake's *Shakespeare and His Times,* 1817.) Vol. II, p. 607.]

WILLIAM WYCHERLEY (1665-6)

He A Wit

He a wit! Hang him; he's only an adopter of straggling jests and fatherless lampoons:

The Plain Dealer (II, 1, 255-256)

FALSTAFF. He a good wit? hang him, baboon! his wit's as thick as Tewksbury mustard;

II Henry IV (II, 4, 261-262)

SIR ROGER L'ESTRANGE (1668)
Too Soon to Think of God

Others there are, that, let a Man advise them upon their *Death-Beds,* and even at the last Gasp, to *send for a Divine,* or to *make some handsom Settlement of their Estates.* Alas, alas! they'll cry; I *have been as bad as this many a time before,* and (with *Falstaff's Hostess*) *I hope in the Lord there's no need to think of him yet.*

Quevedo's *Visions* (First Edition 1688)
London 1708, p. 43

So a' cried out, 'God, God, God!' three or four times. Now I, to comfort him, bid him a' should not think of God; I hoped there was no need to trouble himself with any such thoughts yet.

Henry V (II, 3, 17-21)

Bona Robas and Merry As the Day Is Long

With that a Voice was heard, *Make way there, clear the Passage*: And this was for a *Bevy* of handsom, buxom, Bona Roba's, in their *Caps* and *Feathers,* that came *Dancing, Laughing,* and *Singing* of *Ballads* and *Lampoons,* and as merry as the Day was long.

(op. cit., p. 89)

We knew where the bona robas were and had the best of them all at commandment.

II Henry IV (III, 2, 25-26)

He shows me where the bachelors sit, and there live we as merry as the day is long.

Much Ado About Nothing (II, 1, 52-54)

SIR ROGER L'ESTRANGE (1668)

Much Ado About Nothing

"All is nothing in the World but *Vanity, Imposture,* and *Constraint*; and I will shew thee the Difference between *Things themselves,* and their *Appearances.* To see this Abundance of *Torches,* with the Magnificence of the *Ceremony* and *Attendance,* One would think there should be some mighty matter in the business: But let me assure thee, that all this Pudder comes to no more, than *much ado about Nothing.*

(op. cit., p. 120)

Happy the Child

You have heard of the Old Saying, *Happy is the child whose Father goes to the Devil.*

(op. cit., p. 169)

And happy always was it for that son
Whose father for his hoarding went to hell.

III Henry VI (II, 2, 47-48)

43

THOMAS OTWAY (1676)

Despair And Die

Yes, vile incestuous woman, it is I,
The King; look on me well, despair, and die.

Don Carlos (V, 1, 129-130)

Ghost of Lady Anne rises:
To-morrow in the battle think on me,
And fall thy edgeless sword: despair, and die!

Richard III (V, 3, 162-163)

CAPTAIN WILLIAM HICKES (Hicks) (1677)

A Noble Man once told his Fool, that if he could but tell him what Sir John Falstaffe's cristian name was he'd settle eight pound a year upon him for life, and he should marry the Dairy Maid, who he loved dearly. "Woo't i-faith Lord?" says the fool. 'I will,' says the Lord. 'Swear it, Lord, swear it,' says he: 'I protest I will,' says me Lord. 'Well stay a little then,' says he—'Sir John What?' says he: 'Why, Sir John Falstaff's Christian name: Nay, 'says my Lord, I'll tell you further: his name is Falstaff and he was christened John: now tell me what Sir John Falstaff's Christian name is.' And after he had walked two or three times about the Room my Lord urged him to tell him. 'Prithee, Lord,' says he, 'tell me his name again.' 'Why his name was Falstaff, and he was Christened John: now tell me his Christen name?' At last, after an hour's pausing — 'Now, Lord, I have it, I have it!' says he: 'for I can tell what Sir John Falstaff's Christen name was; and shall I have eight pound a year?' 'Yes, and Doll; I, that thou shalt I protest,' says he agen. 'Why then' says he, 'bear witness, for I have hit on 't now, Sir John Falstaff's Christen name was—he was christened Sir John Falstaff. Look you there, you Rogues, who's the fool now? Hey for Doll! O brave Doll! she's mine own: I'll go buss her now, for she's mine own, you Rogues.'

Coffee House Jests, 1677, pp. 111-112

CHARLES COTTON (1678)

The Whining School-Boy

The slick-fac'd schoolboy satchel takes,
And with slow pace small riddance makes.

The Morning Quatrains (Stanza XVII, 61-64)

And then the whining school-boy, with his satchel
And shining morning face, creeping like snail
Unwillingly to school.

As You Like It (II, 7, 145-147)

THOMAS OTWAY (1682)

Dear As The Ruddy Drops

Once she was dear, indeed; the drops that fell
From my sad heart, when she forgot her duty,
The fountain of my life was not so precious.

Venice Preserved (I, 1, 74-76)

You are my true and honourable wife,
As dear to me as are the ruddy drops
That visit my sad heart.

Julius Caesar (II, 1, 288-290)

THOMAS SHADWELL (1689)

It Were Well To Do It Quickly

When a thing must be done, 'tis best to do it quickly.

Bury Fair (I, 2, 92)

If it were done when 'tis done, then 'twere well
It were done quickly:

Macbeth (I, 7, 1-2)

[Another allusion to *Macbeth* in this play is cited by G. Thorn-Drury, *More Shakespeare Allusions,* 1924, p. 26; also cited by Munro, *Mod. Phil.* XIII, p. 160.]

THE ATHENIAN ORACLE (1703, etc., reprints of 1691-1697)

" 'Tis said, our Nation is *richer* in *Humour* than any in *Europe;* and tho the Stage has large *Supplies* from it, yet it can never never be *exhausted.* If it be so, *Ben. Johnson* stands fairest for *Treasurer,* tho he need not have gone farther than any one of his *Merry Wives of Windsor* to have employ'd him all his Life: He needed but have *shown one Face* in one *Play* to have had sufficient *Variety."*

[The Athenian Oracle: Being an ENTIRE COLLECTION of all the VALUABLE QUESTIONS AND ANSWERS IN THE old *ATHENIAN Mercuries.* (1691-1697) Intermix'd with many CASES in *Divinity, History, Philosophy, Mathematicks, Love, Poetry,* never before *Published.* To which is Added, An *Alphabetical Table* for the Speedy *finding* of any *QUESTIONS.* By a *Member* of the Athenian *SOCIETY. LONDON,* Printed, for Andrew Bell, at the *Cross-Keys* and *Bible,* in *Cornhill,* near *Stocks Market,* 1703. Volume IV, entitled *Athenian Sport,* London, 1707, pp. 93-4.]

"Were I to direct a *Painter* to draw the *Labour in vain,* he shou'd throw aside the old Story of *Lathering* the *Blackamoor,* and instead of it, shou'd paint the *Taming of the Shrew,* which is scarce probable enough to make a *Play* of it, because none can affirm 'tis a true *Image of Life.* An *Opera* indeed might be made on't, such another Business as the *Tempest;* but the Characters wou'd be as incredible, and much stranger than the *two Cubbs* begot by an *Incubus."*

(op. cit., p. 180)

"Tho I'm the *softest Creature in Nature,* yet am I bad Company for Ladies, for they'l fit a whole day in talking of nothing but the *newest Fashions* (and how much they're admir'd by this Beau and t'other Beau) —How can I have Patience to hear this, when I'm positive *there's nothing new?* And when they ask me when I saw any *new Play,* I bluntly tell 'em, there is no such thing: For you know, Madam, and so wou'd they, if they'd look into old Authors, that *Dryden* stole from *Shakespear,* and *Shakespear* from *Ben. Johnson;* and they all so steal from one another, that there's no Wit in any *Play,* but what we had fifty years ago."

(op. cit., p. 335)

"*To swear and forswear,* and to play at fast and loose with a Crown (as a late Author observes) *is no new thing.* Neither is it any *new thing* for Men to cheat, slander, duel, whore; and to pick a Pocket under the Gallows, is a *Custom as old as* Tyburn.— Neither is it a *new thing to see a Man accuse himself* (for a guilty Conscience e'nt easy without it) or for Men of a mean Birth to grow proud, if they grow rich, and to forget their Duty both to God and Man: This is but *Shakespear* and *Ben. Johnson* brought again upon the Stage: And now I talk of Poets, I may venture to say 'tis no *new thing* to see Poets starve.— (*Oldham* cou'd scarce pay for his Garret and a Sunday's Dinner; and for the *famous Butler,* he was kept so *poor,* that *he was forc'd to die and be inter'd on Tick*)—But 'tis no *new thing* to see *Poets* build Castles in the Air; and I'm sure 'tis no *new thing* to see a Chymist spend his Estate in searching after the Philosopher's Stone. . . . . ."

(op. cit., p. 337)

50

GERARD LANGBAINE (1691)

A very ancient Author, who writ a Play in old fashion'd Metre; which he calls *A Lamentable Tragedy,* mixed full of pleasant Mirth; containing the Life of *Cambises* King of *Persia, from the beginning* of his Kingdom unto his Death, his one good deed of *Execution, after the many wicked Deeds,* and tyrannous Murders committed by and through him; and *last of all his odious Death, by Gods Justice appointed. Done in such order as followeth;* printed 4° Lond. —by John Allde. In stead of naming more than *Justin* and *Herodotus,* for the true Story, I shall set down the beginning of this Play, spoke by King *Cambises;* not only to give our Reader a Taste of our Author's Poetry; but because I believe it was this Play *Shakespear* meant, when he brought in Sir *John Falstaff,* speaking in K. *Cambyses* Vein.

An Account of the English Dramatick Poets. Oxford, 1691, p. 408.

Give me a cup of sack to make my eyes look red, that it may be thought I have wept; for I must speak in passion, and I will do it in King Cambyses' vein.

I Henry IV (II, 4, 422-426)

[This allusion appears to have been overlooked by Munro II, 355, and by G. Thorn-Drury, though the latter in *More Seventeenth Century Allusions,* 1924, prints seven passages (p. 30) overlooked by Munro.]

51

THE ATHENIAN MERCURY (1693)

"All Sacred Truth, tho' staring Mortals wonder!
  If but once compared with you he be,
  Is a meer A T H E N I A N in Poetry.
Nay, the Wayward Sisters who in *Macbeth* strove
Which shou'd best their Art in reading Fortunes
        prove,
Had yielded their *Rosin,* and *Beesoms,* and *Devils*
        to you,
Who twenty times stranger Feats can do:
Finally, Ne'er was seen a Monster half so rare
At the *Bell-savage Inn,* or old *Bartholomew-Fair."*

[*The Doggerel Mercury,* Saturday, June 10, 1693. *Athenian Mercury,* X, no. 22.]

WILLIAM CONGREVE (1695)

At the Turning of the Tide

And d'ye hear, bring me, let me see—within a quarter
of twelve—hem—he, hem!—just upon the turning of
the tide, bring me the urinal.

Love for Love (III, 13, 10-13)

A' parted even just between twelve and one, even
at the turning o' the tide:

Henry V (II, 3, 12-14)

MATTHEW PRIOR (1696)

Murdering Sleep

What measures shall poor Paulo keep
With madam in this piteous taking?
She, like Macbeth, has murdered sleep,
And won't allow him rest through waking.

Paulo Purganti and His Wife (ll. 123-126)

Methought I heard a voice cry, 'Sleep no more!
Macbeth does murder sleep.' . . . .

Macbeth (II, 2, 36-37)

DR. SAMUEL GARTH (1699)

An Apothecary

His shop the gazing vulgar's eyes employs,
With foreign trinkets and domestic toys,
Here mummies lay, most reverently stale,
And there the tortoise hung her coat of mail:
Not far from some huge shark's devouring head,
The flying fish their finny pinions spread:
Aloft, in rows large poppy-heads were strung,
And near, a scaly alligator hung:
In this place drugs, in musty heaps decay'd:
In that, dry'd bladders, and drawn teeth are laid.

The Dispensary, Transversed, or the consult of Physicians, a poem in six cantos. London, 1701. Canto II.

And in his needy shop a tortoise hung,
An alligator stuff'd, and other skins
Of ill-shaped fishes; and about his shelves
A beggarly account of empty boxes,
Green earthen pots, bladders and musty seeds,
Remnants of packthread and old cakes of roses,
Were thinly scatter'd to make up a show.

Romeo and Juliet (V, 1, 42-48)

[Dodd, in his *Beauties of Shakespeare,* 1752 (II, 217) writes: "Garth, in his dispensary, hath endeavoured to imitate this excellent description of Shakespear's: the lines themselves will be best proof of his success."]

NICHOLAS ROWE (1700)

This Goodly Frame, This Canopy

If Love be monstrous, so is this fair Frame,
This beauteous World, this Canopy, the Sky;
That sparkling shines with Gems of Light innumer-
      able:
And so art thou and I, since Love made all;
Who kindly reconcil'd the jarring Atoms
In friendly League, and bid 'em be a World.

The Ambitious Step-Mother (V, 2, 70-75)

This goodly frame, the earth, seems to me a sterile
promontory, this most excellent canopy, the air, look
you, this brave o'erhanging firmament, this majesti-
cal roof fretted with golden fire, why, it appears no
other thing to me than a foul and pestilent congrega-
tion of vapours.

Hamlet (II, 2, 310-315)

W. AYLOFFE (1701)

Why should we step back to Beaumont and Fletcher, to Shakespear and Ben Johnson? We have later proof (tho' not greater) of the English Genius; We have the Utile dulci, the natural and sublime.

[*Poetical Works of Sir Charles Sedley,* London, Second Edition, 1707. ("Preface to the Reader," by W. Ayloffe, written 1701, First Edition, 1702; 1707, A3.)]

INDEX I

INDEX II

INDEX III

58